Read All About

SOCCER

by Colette Weil Parrinello

PEBBLE
a capstone imprint

Published by Pebble, an imprint of Capstone
1710 Roe Crest Drive, North Mankato, Minnesota 56003
capstonepub.com

Library of Congress Cataloging-in-Publication Data
Names: Weil Parrinello, Colette, author.
Title: Read all about soccer / by Colette Weil Parrinello.
Description: North Mankato, Minnesota : Pebble, an imprint of Capstone, [2023] | Series: Read all about it | Includes index. | Audience: Ages 5-8 | Audience: Grades K-1 | Summary: "Did you know a soccer field is called a pitch? Or that only soccer goalkeepers can use their hands? Find out all about soccer positions, moves, equipment, teams, and more in this fact-filled book. Stunning photos give readers an up-close look at soccer players in action"— Provided by publisher.
Identifiers: LCCN 2022025103 (print) | LCCN 2022025104 (ebook) | ISBN 9780756572693 (hardcover) | ISBN 9780756573430 (paperback) | ISBN 9780756572662 (pdf) | ISBN 9780756572686 (kindle edition)
Subjects: LCSH: Soccer—Juvenile literature.
Classification: LCC GV943.25 W45 2023 (print) | LCC GV943.25 (ebook) | DDC 796.334—dc23
LC record available at https://lccn.loc.gov/2022025103
LC ebook record available at https://lccn.loc.gov/2022025104

Editorial Credits
Editor: Carrie Sheely; Designer: Bobbie Nuytten; Media Researcher: Jo Miller; Production Specialist: Tori Abraham

Printed and bound in China. PO 5130

Table of Contents

Words in **bold** are in the glossary.

Chapter 1

History of Soccer

Soccer is one of the oldest sports. In ancient times, people played games that were like soccer. Today, soccer is played in more than 200 countries.

More than 4,000 years ago, ancient Greeks played the soccer-like game episkyros. Teams kicked the ball and used their hands to score goals.

In ancient China, soldiers played a game like soccer called Ts'u-chü or Cuju. They kicked a leather ball into a net.

Early soccer balls were made from inflated pig bladders and strips of leather.

In 1863, England's Football Association (FA) created soccer's first official rules.

The first women's soccer teams formed in the late 1880s in the United Kingdom.

In 1904, FA members formed the Federation Internationale de Football Association (FIFA). FIFA organizes the World Cups and other major international **tournaments.**

England played Scotland in the world's first international soccer match in 1872.

INTERNATIONAL FOOT-BALL MATCH, (ASSOCIATION RULES,) ENGLAND v. SCOTLAND, WEST OF SCOTLAND CRICKET GROUND, HAMILTON CRESCENT, PARTICK, SATURDAY, 30th November, 1872, at 2 p.m. ADMISSION—ONE SHILLING.

More people watch soccer in person and on TV than any other sport.

Outside of Canada, the United States, and Australia, soccer is called football.

Chapter 2

Playing on a Field

A soccer game is played on a field, or **pitch**. Players try to put the ball into the other team's net to score. The team with the highest number of goals at the end of the game wins.

The pitch is usually grass. Artificial grass is rarely used in professional games.

A goal is scored when the ball crosses the other team's goal line between the goal posts and under the **crossbar**.

Each soccer team has 11 players on the field at a time.

A **header** is using the head to pass the ball or aim it into the goal.

Cristiano Ronaldo once jumped 9.5 feet (2.9 meters) to head the ball into the goal!

9

Players can touch the ball with their feet, legs, body, and head. Only the goalkeepers can use their hands.

The bicycle kick is an amazing move in which a player moves their upper body backward and pedals the legs to strike the ball in midair.

Referees make sure players are following the rules. They watch for **fouls**.

A yellow card from the referee is a warning for a player's misconduct.

A red card means a player must leave the pitch immediately and is not replaced.

11

Chapter 3

Players and Positions

Each player has an important job to do.
The four main positions are goalkeepers,
defenders, midfielders, and forwards.

Forwards score the
most goals. The
center forward is
called the striker.

Midfielders play between
the forwards and defenders.

Midfielders run up and down the field. Sometimes they run more than 7 miles (11 kilometers) in a game!

Defenders block attacking forwards.

The goalkeeper keeps balls out of the goal.

Star goalkeeper Briana Scurry played for the U.S. women's national team. In 2017, she was inducted into the National Soccer Hall of Fame.

When the goalkeeper keeps the other team from scoring any goals in a game, it's called a clean sheet. Goalkeeper Hope Solo holds the record for the most "clean sheets," 102, in U.S. women's soccer.

A player's uniform, or kit, is a jersey, shorts, shin guards, knee-high socks, and cleats.

Goalkeepers wear gloves to protect their hands and grip the ball.

Goalkeepers wear a different color uniform from the rest of their team and the opposing team.

Star forward Marta Vieira da Silva became the first soccer player to score in five straight Olympic Games.

Chapter 4

Teams

Most communities have youth clubs and teams. Many players continue in high school and college. A few play professionally and earn money.

There are about 3,900 professional clubs. Mexico has the most with more than 260.

Real Madrid was named the best soccer club of the 20th century by FIFA.

Famous **rivalries** are between Real Madrid and FC Barcelona and England's Manchester United and Liverpool.

Most professional clubs run youth academies to identify and train players starting from age 6. By 13, the best players are invited to stay.

Argentinian superstar Lionel Messi was **scouted** for FC Barcelona's famous La Masia youth academy at 13 years old.

In 2022, midfielder Maximo Carrizo became the youngest player to sign a pro contract with Major League Soccer (MLS) at age 14.

Countries select their best players for their national team.

Brazil has the most successful men's national team.

The United States has the most successful women's national team.

The club that has won the most trophies is Egypt's Al Ahly with 188.

Chapter 5

Fans and Stadiums

Soccer fans shout and sing to cheer on their favorite teams. They're proud of their stadiums and show support for teams in many ways.

✳ In the 1930s, soccer fans in the United Kingdom started wearing handmade scarves in team colors. Today, soccer scarves are still popular.

The vuvuzela is a popular cheering horn at South African games. But it was so loud at the 2010 World Cup that it was **banned** from future World Cups.

The Maracanã Stadium in Brazil set a record for the most people ever attending a soccer game during the 1950 World Cup. It held 173,850 people!

Nef Stadium in Turkey holds the record for the loudest crowd roar. The crowd of 52,044 fans was as loud as a jet taking off.

Before a match, professional teams enter a stadium with youth players who are specially chosen.

One of the largest stadiums is Camp Nou in Barcelona, Spain. It holds 99,354 people.

The shape of the First National Bank (FNB) Stadium in Johannesburg, South Africa, was inspired by traditional African pots called calabashes.

You can only get to Ottmar Hitzfeld Gspon Arena, Switzerland, by cable car because it is 6,562 feet (2,000 m) above sea level.

The outside of the Allianz Arena in Munich, Germany, has 3,000 panels that change color.

Chapter 6

Mascots and Nicknames

Mascots add to the fun of a game.
Many teams have fun nicknames too.

England's Arsenal team has a mascot named Gunnersaurus. It is a 7-foot (2.1-meter) dinosaur.

Germany's FC Cologne mascot is a live billy goat.

Spain's Villarreal CF nickname is "Yellow Submarine" from the Beatles song and their team color.

On July 4, 2016, the LA Galaxy's mascot Cozmo jumped out of an airplane and parachuted into the StubHub Center in California.

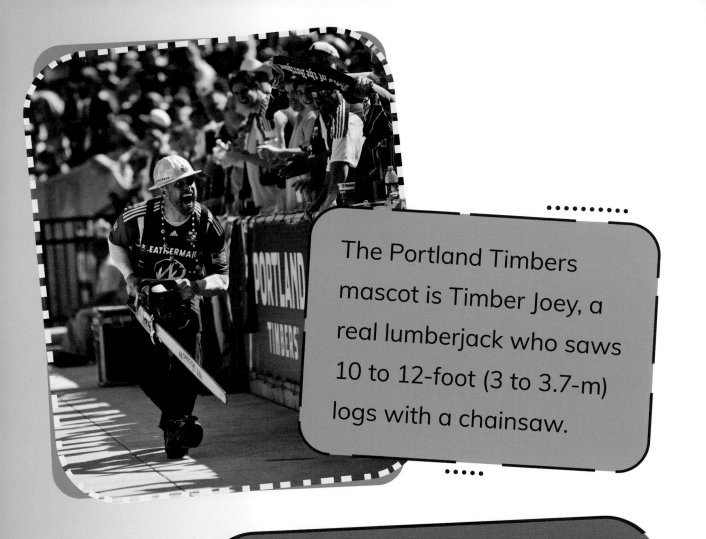

The Portland Timbers mascot is Timber Joey, a real lumberjack who saws 10 to 12-foot (3 to 3.7-m) logs with a chainsaw.

Japan's national team nickname is the Samurai Blue for the players' deep blue uniforms.

Australia's national team nickname, Socceroos, is a combination of the words "soccer" and "kangaroos."

The Netherlands national team is known as Clockwork Orange. Fans wear orange and their mascot is an orange lion.

Brazil's national team has a yellow canary mascot with an angry face. Its face shows the frustration of fans after losing the World Cup in 2014.

Chapter 7

World Cups

FIFA World Cups are some of the largest competitions in sports worldwide. Held every four years, countries participate with their national team.

The first World Cup was held in 1930 in Uruguay.

The Women's World Cup is held the year after the Men's World Cup.

The first Women's World Cup was held in 1991 in China.

Nearly half the world, 3.57 billion people, watched the 2018 World Cup on TV.

The highest-scoring game in World Cup history took place in 1954. Austria won against Switzerland, 7-5.

The 2002 World Cup was the first to be hosted by two countries. Both South Korea and Japan hosted it.

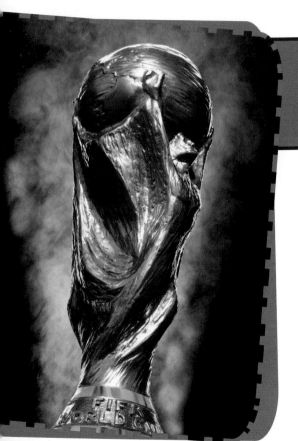

The winners of the World Cup receive a large gold trophy.

Banned items at World Cups have included selfie sticks, tablets, cameras, inflatable balls, umbrellas, and chewing gum.

The FIFAe World Cup is a large online e-sports tournament. Gamers compete to win prize money.

Glossary

ban—to not allow

crossbar—a bar that connects to both posts of the soccer goal

foul—an action that is against the rules

header—a shot or pass in soccer using the head; children 10 years and under cannot do headers

pitch—a soccer field

rivalry—a fierce feeling of competition between two teams

scout—to look for players who might be able to join a team

tournament—a series of matches between several players or teams, ending in one winner

Index

photo credit: Di Starr Studios

About the Author

Colette Weil Parrinello is a writer, runner, and avid reader. She loves sports and the outdoors. She lives under the majestic redwoods in Northern California and can be seen running the paths along the marsh and bay.